Punctuation Book one

T. G. Ledgard M.A.

Deputy Headmaster, Sheldon School,
Chippenham

Cassell

CASSELL LTD.
1 St. Anne's Road, Eastbourne,
East Sussex BN21 3UN

First published 1977
Seventh impression 1982
Eighth impression 1985
Ninth impression 1986

ISBN 0 304 29771 2

Printed in Hong Kong

Contents

Introduction

For some time now the emphasis in the teaching of written English has been on free personal expression and creative writing. While these must be the most worthwhile of all written English activities, they have been pursued in many cases at the expense of good handwriting, careful spelling and correct punctuation. Many adults—including parents, employers and heads of English departments in secondary schools—feel that today's pupils do not receive the basic grounding in mechanical accuracy which is necessary for good written English.

This series of four books, a systematic punctuation course designed for regular use in the secondary (or middle) school, is intended to meet a need which will become increasingly obvious as the pendulum swings back towards a greater concern for correct English.

The books are written in the simplest possible way, avoiding all but the most common and easily understood grammatical terms, yet they cover all punctuation marks in all their usages. The series is so arranged that, if desired, 'Punctuation 1' could be used for first years in secondary schools, 'Punctuation 2' for second years, and so on. There are carefully compiled and graded exercises on all punctuation marks as well as a large number of revision exercises.

Correct punctuation is just as important as correct spelling and easily legible handwriting. Pupils who are taken through this series in a systematic way will gain a thorough understanding of something that is an essential element of good written English.

Full stop

Reading is like driving a car or riding a bicycle. For some of the time you go smoothly along but every now and then you have to stop. When you are driving or cycling, you have a STOP sign or red traffic light to make sure you stop at the end of a road and don't have an accident. These are the most important of all road signs.

In reading you have a stop sign as well. It is called the FULL STOP (.) and there must be one at the end of every sentence. Of all punctuation marks it is the most important. Whenever you see one, you must stop. If you take no notice of the full stop and go straight on, you will have an accident with your reading just as you would with a car or a bicycle.

Look at these two letters. This is what Alison wrote to one of her friends, Bill:

> Dear Bill,
> I hope you are free this Saturday we are having a real party on Tuesday we got permission to use the hall so we shall have plenty of room and be able to make a lot of noise without disturbing anyone. I hope you will let me know when the party is over we can come back here and play some records.
> Yours,
> Alison

Alison's mother read the letter and found it hard to understand. She explained to Alison about full stops and helped her correct it. The letter ended up like this:

> Dear Bill,
>   I hope you are free this Saturday.
> We are having a real party. On Tuesday we
> got permission to use the hall so we
> shall have plenty of room and be able to
> make a lot of noise without disturbing
> anyone. I hope you will let me know. When
> the party is over we can come back here
> and play some records.
>   Yours,
>   Alison

It is quite impossible to read the first letter easily and to understand it. We don't know where to stop because some of the full stops have been left out. When Alison has been shown how to use full stops properly and she puts them in the right places, as she does in the second letter, then it is much more straightforward to read and we can understand it.

It is most important that, when you write, you put full stops in the right places. Otherwise what you write will be very difficult to read.

You must put a full stop (or question mark or exclamation mark) at the end of every sentence.

To put full stops in the right place, therefore, you have to remember what a sentence is.

A sentence is a group of words which makes complete sense by itself.

For example, if you went up to someone and said *a dirty face* or *walking down the street*, they would not know what you meant. These groups of words mean nothing by themselves and so they are not sentences.

But you could say *My dog is called William*. That group
of words makes complete sense by itself and is
therefore a sentence.

Exercise 1:

Some of the groups of words below are sentences
(because they make complete sense by themselves).
Write out only these groups, remembering to put a full
stop at the end of each sentence.

Example: *You may start now*
becomes *You may start now*.

(a)   My chair squeaks
(b)   Scoring a goal
(c)   Motor-bikes are very dangerous machines
(d)   This is nonsense
(e)   Litter lying on the classroom floor
(f)   The manager of the team
(g)   She bought a new pair of shoes
(h)   Buying a new pair of shoes
(i)   These shoes are new
(j)   Smart new shoes

Exercise 2:

Do as you did in exercise 1.

(a)   Go away
(b)   My brother, the famous acrobat
(c)   Having eaten the last biscuit
(d)   Please sit down
(e)   A large black handbag, lying on the path
(f)   William opened his eyes
(g)   It seems that the rain will never stop
(h)   Because I saw him on Saturday
(i)   An old man, sitting in the sun
(j)   I have finished

Each sentence must begin with a capital letter. Whenever you start a new sentence, make sure that the first letter you write is a capital letter.

Exercise 3:

Some of the groups of words below are sentences (because they make complete sense by themselves). Write out only these groups of words. Remember that you must put a capital letter at the beginning and a full stop at the end of each sentence.

Example: *dogs like bones*
becomes *Dogs like bones.*

(a) singing in the bath
(b) a house on a cliff overlooking the sea
(c) my dog can jump a six-foot fence
(d) quite out of control
(e) the clock has stopped at ten to four
(f) don't drop that tray
(g) you will regret it
(h) although he is a good worker
(i) the fat man ate twenty-seven pancakes
(j) a thrush sitting on four blue eggs

Exercise 4:

Do as you did in exercise 3.

(a) the bomb narrowly missed the hidden commandos
(b) in spite of the heavy rain we have had recently
(c) help me
(d) a table with lots of books on it
(e) squealing like a dying pig
(f) carefully he took aim
(g) a race-horse that just won't race
(h) when the guard was looking the other way
(i) two strawberry ice-creams, please
(j) only at the last moment did the lorry swerve aside

Exercise 5:

Write out the words below, making them into five sentences by adding only full stops and capital letters. Do not start each sentence on a new line.

Ann was not feeling very happy she didn't know many of the other children suddenly through the door came her mother she smiled at Ann it was time to go home

Exercise 6:

Do as you did in exercise 5. This time there are ten sentences.

first you must work out what you are going to write about then take a clean sheet of paper in the top right-hand corner put your name in the top left-hand corner write the date leave two lines in the middle of the next line write the title of your story you may then begin to write remember to start each new paragraph at least an inch in from the margin write very neatly when you have finished check carefully what you have written

To say that a sentence is a group of words which makes complete sense by itself is not, however, quite enough. It works very well if all the sentences are simple ones. Sometimes, though, a sentence has several parts, for example:

The dog slept quietly in his basket while the burglar was stealing the money.

If we follow the rule we have used so far, we would put a full stop after *The dog slept*. These words make complete sense by themselves.

But, if we do this, we are left with the words, *quietly in his basket while the burglar was stealing the money*. These words do not make sense by themselves; they do not form a sentence and we cannot have parts of sentences left over. The only way we can make sense of these words is by adding them to the first group of words, *The dog slept*. This gives us a complete sentence:

> *The dog slept quietly in his basket while the burglar was stealing the money.*

So we have to add something to our first definition of a sentence. A sentence is a group of words which makes complete sense by itself, **but it may be necessary to add other groups of words which cannot stand as sentences on their own.**

Exercise 7:

Some of the groups of words below are two sentences and some are only one. Write out each group, adding full stops and capital letters, to show clearly whether there is one sentence or two.

Example: *play that record again it's good*
becomes *Play that record again. It's good.*

(a) I can't eat this meat it's far too tough
(b) she had coloured her eyelids with bright green eye-shadow
(c) there was a strong wind the washing was dry in less than an hour
(d) James won the toss he decided he would play against the wind
(e) leave me alone
(f) the teacher was angry that Susan had cheated and he told her off sternly
(g) I like bananas but not when they are green
(h) don't do that it's dangerous
(i) the boy waited for his friend but he never turned up
(j) the fish fought hard it took two and a half hours to land it

Exercise 8:

Some of the groups of words below are one sentence;
some are two or more. Write out each group, adding
full stops and capital letters where they are needed.

(a) he was over six feet tall and very strong
(b) come in sit down have a cigarette
(c) the fire burned fiercely soon the factory was
     nothing but a smouldering heap of glowing rubble
(d) when there is thunder my grandmother hides under
     the blankets
(e) you can easily tell the difference between
     blackbirds and starlings blackbirds bounce
     starlings strut
(f) the car spun off the track the driver was thrown
     clear he landed in the long grass he was unhurt
(g) Henry did not feel well he had eaten the coin his
     mother had put in the Christmas pudding
(h) suddenly there came a loud hissing noise from the
     kitchen Angela had forgotten all about the milk she
     was heating it had boiled over
(i) he had forgotten to take the cap off the lens of his
     camera so the picture did not come out
(j) the thief felt a hand on his shoulder he spun round
     and found himself looking into the steady gaze of a
     large policeman

Exercise 9:

Write out the following, adding only full stops and
capital letters. You should have five sentences when
you have finished.

please fasten your seat-belts and extinguish all
cigarettes we shall be landing at New York in ten
minutes we are told that the weather at the airport is dry
but cloudy the time in New York now is twenty-three
minutes past eleven I hope you have had a pleasant
flight and that we shall see you again

Exercise 10:

Do as you did in exercise 9. You should have five sentences when you have finished.

it is silly to say that you do not like teachers teachers are just people some of them are nice and some are not so nice in this school most of them are very reasonable and they do try to help the pupils I think that you are angry with teachers only because you have just been punished

Exercise 11:

Do as you did in exercise 9. You should have ten sentences when you have finished.

my brother is just three years old I am very fond of him really but he can be a nuisance yesterday I was in the kitchen cutting up some meat for a pie when my mother called out that Jackie was on the phone covering up the meat I left the kitchen and spent about five minutes talking to Jackie I came back to see my brother feeding the last piece of meat to the dog who was gratefully licking his lips I gave a shout but it was too late to do anything just then my mother came in to see how my cooking was getting on I was a bit worried about what she would say when she heard what had happened she listened to me in silence while I explained when I had finished she told me quietly that my brother was too young to be blamed and that it was all my fault

Exercise 12:

Do as you did in exercise 9. You should have ten sentences when you have finished.

my first job was with a vet and my first morning was a sad one after I had put on my overall I opened the door of the waiting room the first person to come in to the surgery was an old man in his arms was a thin and blind terrier who seemed even older than his master in a trembling voice the old man told us that he wanted the dog put to sleep they had been together for seventeen years but now the dog could hardly walk and he seemed to be in constant pain the old man felt it would be kinder to have him put down as he handed his dog to the vet the old man's eyes filled with tears then he turned and shuffled out of the surgery door the dog whimpered softly in the vet's arms

Capital letters for proper names

PROPER NAMES are names of particular people, particular places, particular times and particular things (especially titles of books etc.).

For example:

People. *Christopher* and *Doctor Sinclair* (but not *the boy* and *the doctor*).

Places. *New Zealand* and *the Pacific Ocean* (but not *the country* and *the ocean*).

Times. *Monday* and *August* (but not *the day* and *the month*).

Things. *Spitfire* and *King Street* (but not *the aeroplane* and *the street*).

Titles. *Beano* and *Top of the Pops* (but not *the comic* and *the pop show*).

Proper names begin with a capital letter.

Note that in titles we do not begin a word like *the, a, to, of, from,* with a capital letter unless it is the first word in the title, e.g. *The Adventures of Tarzan.*

Describing words formed from proper names nearly always begin with a capital letter, e.g. *French, Indian, Christian.*

Exercise 13:

Write out the sentences below, using capital letters where they are needed. Remember that the word *I* is always written as a capital letter and that sentences always begin with a capital letter too.

Example: *the wilken family went to butlins.*
becomes *The Wilken family went to Butlins*.

(a) fiona and helen have gone to aberdeen today.
(b) last wednesday the school was addressed by sir robert sims.
(c) william defeated harold at the battle of hastings in 1066.
(d) after a fierce battle the english were finally beaten by the french.
(e) the two countries signed a treaty of friendship.
(f) the common market began with the treaty of rome in 1956.
(g) madrid is the capital city of spain.
(h) my favourite television programmes are crossroads and the golden shot.
(i) one of mark's favourite books was the wind in the willows.
(j) i am cross because mrs. morris has just driven her dirty old ford over my foot.

Question mark

A QUESTION MARK (?) at the end of a sentence shows that a question has been asked. The rule is:

If a sentence asks a question, you must place a question mark at the end. A question mark stands instead of a full stop and must be followed by a capital letter.

Example: *Do you think it is cruel to keep animals in zoos?*

Exercise 14:

Some of the sentences below are questions. They need a question mark at the end. The others are not, and so need a full stop at the end. Write out each sentence, adding the correct punctuation mark.

Examples: *Some one has let my tyres down*
becomes *Someone has let my tyres down.*
But *Who has let my tyres down*
becomes *Who has let my tyres down?*

(a) Can you touch your toes without bending your knees

(b) The duck pecked Fred's finger when he gave it some bread

(c) Where can we park our caravan

(d) Why are you using such an ugly colour of nail varnish

(e) The boat rocked wildly in the heavy swell

(f) I like school food better than the food we have at home

(g)   Did you have a good holiday
(h)   Have a good holiday
(i)   Please tell me the time
(j)   What is the time

You must be specially careful with some sentences which sound like questions but which are really not.

Ted asked the referee how much longer there was until the end of the match.

This may sound like a question but, if you think about it clearly, you will realise that it is a statement. It tells us what Ted said; it does not ask a question. You need a question mark only if you are writing down the actual question:

How much longer is there until the end of the match?

Exercise 15:

Do as you did in exercise 14. Work out carefully whether each sentence is a question or a statement.

Examples: *I can see why she is so popular with the boys*
becomes *I can see why she is so popular with the boys.*
But *Why is she so popular with the boys*
becomes *Why is she so popular with the boys?*

(a)   Why are you being so nasty to me
(b)   The little girl asked how much the doll cost
(c)   Uncle Kenneth asked the small boy if he was lost
(d)   What is the capital of Peru
(e)   Please can we have our ball back
(f)   I know a man who keeps an eel in his bath
(g)   The king asked why the admiral had lost so many
       ships
(h)   Please stop asking questions
(i)   Who was the first man to land on the moon
(j)   Michael wondered when Julia would turn up

Exclamation mark

An exclamation is a sharp expression, usually of strong feeling, often surprise. It may be one word or it may be a sentence. After an exclamation you must use an EXCLAMATION MARK (!). The rule is:

> **You must use an exclamation mark after an exclamation. An exclamation mark stands instead of a full stop and must be followed by a capital letter.**

It is often up to you to decide if you need an exclamation mark or a full stop. It depends whether you think you are making an exclamation or not. *I have just seen an elephant in the street* would be an exclamation in Birmingham and so would be written *I have just seen an elephant in the street!* However, in an Indian village it would probably not be an exclamation and so would end with a full stop, *I have just seen an elephant in the street.*

In general, do not use too many exclamation marks. Sentences like *It is a lovely day.* are not really exclamations and should have only a full stop at the end.

These are the times when you **must** use an exclamation mark:

A. Sentences (not questions) beginning with *What* or *How* are always exclamations and so will always end in an exclamation mark, e.g. *What a pretty girl!* or *How silly you are!*

Exercise 16:

Punctuate the following sentences correctly, adding only full stops, question marks and exclamation marks.

(a) How hot it was yesterday
(b) How hot was it yesterday
(c) I do like chocolates
(d) What big teeth you have, Grandmother
(e) How clever of Miss Richards to remember my birthday
(f) How clever is Miss Richards
(g) Peter is such a good worker
(h) What a stupid mistake
(i) What a clumsy girl you are
(j) What have you broken now

B. Short and sudden exclamations, standing by themselves, e.g. *Look out!* or *Help!* or *Good heavens!* or *Oh!* You can often, though, make these exclamations part of a sentence and so you will have a choice of punctuation, e.g.

> *Good heavens! We have run over a dog!*
or *Good heavens, we have run over a dog!*
but **never** *Good heavens! we have run over a dog!*

Why is the last example wrong? Remember the rule: An exclamation mark stands instead of a full stop and must be followed by a capital letter.

C. When somebody's name is called by itself and not as part of a sentence, e.g. *John!* As in B above you could have.

> *John! Come here!*
or *John, come here!**
but **never** *John! come here!*

* See page 23 for an explanation of this comma.

(You do not have to put an exclamation mark, as we have done, after *dog* and *here* in the sentences on p. 19. You might wish to use a full stop instead. It is up to you.)

Exercise 17:

Do as you did in exercise 16.

(a) Dad Your tea is ready
(b) How beautiful the view is
(c) Come quickly
(d) My word That was a near miss
(e) How can you tell the age of a tree
(f) Oh dear She must have missed her train again
(g) Stephen is such a polite boy
(h) Look where you are going
(i) Bonzo Come here at once
(j) What an interesting experiment

Comma

The COMMA (,) is used in a number of different ways, but always to separate words or groups of words from each other. It is not, however, as strong as a full stop, which is used to separate one sentence from another. It should **never** be used instead of a full stop.

The comma placed between items in a list

A comma is placed between items in a list instead of *and* or *or*.

To write *Mother bought bread and butter and tea and salt and sugar.* would be very clumsy. Instead you would write
Mother bought bread, butter, tea, salt and sugar.
Every *and* except the last one has been replaced by a comma.

Exercise 18:

In the following sentences replace each *and* and each *or*, except the last one in the sentence, by commas.

Example: *The park was full of oaks and elms and birches and willows.*
becomes *The park was full of oaks, elms, birches and willows.*

(a) Andrews and Jones and Evans and Dimmock will report to the Headmaster after assembly.
(b) In the last year my sister has had measles and mumps and chicken pox.

(c) The field had turned into an ugly heap of old tyres and rusting metal and broken glass.
(d) Would you like coffee or tea or milk or orange?
(e) I managed to find Mr. Peckham and Mrs. Davidson and Miss Williams but not young Alexander.
(f) The flying acrobats and tumbling clowns and almost human monkeys and beautiful horses and enormous elephants made it a circus to remember.
(g) Flour and milk and butter and sugar and eggs and raisins are the main ingredients.
(h) The room was full of dust and cobwebs and dead spiders and dead flies.
(i) Matthew and Mark and Luke and John wrote the Gospels.
(j) She was not sure whether she wanted to learn to play the piano or the guitar or the violin or the recorder or the mouth organ.

The list need not be a list of things. Here are some other examples:

A. *He was a tall, thin, bald, worried-looking man.*
(Instead of *He was a tall and thin and bald and worried-looking man.*) This is a very common kind of list where you have a number of words (*tall, thin, bald, worried-looking*) describing something (*man*).

B. *The teacher asked, ordered, begged and threatened the boy but he would not apologise.*
(Instead of *The teacher asked and ordered and begged and threatened the boy but he would not apologise.*) This is a list of actions.

C. *You may watch television only when you have had your tea, taken the dog for a walk, done your homework and tidied your room.*
(Instead of *You may watch television only when you have had your tea and taken the dog for a walk and done your homework and tidied your room.*) This is a list of different groups of words.

In all these examples the same rule applies: a comma is placed between items in a list instead of *and* or *or*.

Exercise 19:

Place commas where necessary in the following sentences.

(a) The mother was sobbing over her small thin weak crying child.
(b) The slave was set free because he was honest and loyal because he had never complained and because he had always worked hard.
(c) The house that burnt down was made of wood that was old dry thin and rotten.
(d) My father loves his family is kind to animals helps old ladies across the road and gives pennies to beggars.
(e) It was a hot sticky thundery threatening day.
(f) Big Aunt Bertha loves to eat spaghetti ravioli lasagne macaroni and all forms of pasta.
(g) He returned the ball hard low fast and straight into the gloves of the wicket-keeper.
(h) The tramp set off with a song in his heart a smile on his lips and his knapsack on his back.
(i) The doctor had an old wise kind face.
(j) Shall we play tennis go for a ride have a swim or just lie in the sun?

The comma used to mark off a term of address

This is a very simple use of the comma. To address someone is to call them by their name. When you do this, the name must be separated from the rest of the sentence by a comma. The rule is:

A term of address is always separated from the rest of the sentence by a comma.

Here are two examples:

Simon, you cannot leave the table until you have finished your meal.
Good morning, Mr. Brown.

Simon is the term of address in the first sentence and *Mr. Brown* in the second. In each case the term of address is separated from the rest of the sentence by a comma, after *Simon* and before *Mr. Brown*.
If the term of address comes in the middle of the sentence, then you must place commas on each side of it, e.g.

Stop barking, Towser, and lie down.

Exercise 20:

Place commas in the following sentences where necessary.

Example: *Can I help you madam?*
becomes *Can I help you, madam?*

(a) What are you doing Jane?
(b) Mr. President I wish to resign.
(c) Darling will you marry me?
(d) You told me on Friday Mr. Simpson that you would be here on time.
(e) I beg your pardon sir.
(f) No Mrs. Wotherspoon I never said that.
(g) Do not be so silly boy.
(h) Mr. Chairman ladies and gentlemen it is indeed an honour to speak to you today.
(i) Dr. Livingstone I presume.
(j) Today my friends is a great occasion.

The worst mistake

The worst mistake that you can make in punctuation is to use a comma at the end of a sentence instead of a full stop. This is often done but it is quite wrong. It shows the writer to be someone who doesn't know what good English is. Remember:

Commas are not full stops.

This is what Michael wrote:

> Mum woke me just after seven, I had my breakfast and went round to Bill's, we walked to school, it was raining.

This is very bad English. Michael has done what many people do—he has used commas at the end of sentences instead of full stops. He should have written:

> Mum woke me just after seven. I had my breakfast and went round to Bill's. We walked to school. It was raining.

Do not make this mistake yourself. Remember:

Commas are not full stops.

Revision exercises

Full stop

Revision exercise 1 (this exercise can be done when you have worked up to page 8):

Some of the groups of words below are sentences (because they make complete sense by themselves). Write out only these groups of words, remembering to put a capital letter at the beginning and a full stop at the end of each sentence.

Example: *the nurse smiled sweetly at the patient* becomes *The nurse smiled sweetly at the patient.*

(a) the squirrel cleaned its paws in the sunshine
(b) be quiet
(c) falling off his bicycle on to the hard pavement
(d) if you steal you will be punished
(e) although he tried his hardest
(f) a lady with a strong personality, greatly respected by all
(g) his fans, all young girls, gave him a real fright
(h) a return ticket to London, please
(i) white dots flashing on the television screen
(j) the best dog in the show

Revision exercise 2 (page 9):

Write out the words below, making them into five sentences by adding only full stops and capital letters. Do not start each sentence on a new line.

Richmond had killed his friend in a fit of anger that was six years ago since then he had been in prison he hated prison Richmond wished he had been hanged

Revision exercise 3 (page 9):

Do as you did in revision exercise 2.

boil a pan of water take an egg place it gently in the boiling water take it out after exactly six minutes you now have a well-boiled egg ready for eating

Revision exercise 4 (page 10):

Some of the groups of words below are two sentences and some are only one. Write out each group, adding full stops and capital letters to show clearly whether there is one sentence or two.

Example: *the fisherman sat patiently on the bank he had caught nothing all day*
becomes *The fisherman sat patiently on the bank. He had caught nothing all day.*

(a) I am not giving you the money for the pop concert you will have to earn it

(b) all the trees bend in that direction because of the westerly wind

(c) the noise of the passing traffic was terrible three families had left the street already

(d) Stephen was a quiet boy he was the only child of an ordinary family living in a council house on a rather ramshackle estate

(e) unless we have some rain I am very much afraid that the harvest will be a poor one

(f) go away I am reading

(g) come back only when you have finished your work

(h) I swallowed a mouthful of water I thought I was drowning

(i) Eric and Maria skated beautifully they glided over the ice with their heads in the air

(j) we had far too much homework last night

Revision exercise 5 (page 11):

Some of the groups of words below are one sentence;
some are two or more. Write out each group, adding
full stops and capital letters where they are needed.

(a) my foot was on the pedestrian crossing you should
     have stopped
(b) smoking is foolish it damages your health it costs
     money
(c) he thought he could carry the heavy tray but he
     had not staggered five steps before he dropped it
     on the floor his mother was very cross
(d) I have warned the President that if he does not
     remove his aircraft carrier from the area we shall
     have to sink it
(e) the house was deserted no one had lived there for
     years
(f) I found the purse in your locker Sheila says she
     saw you take it I think it is time you told the truth
(g) you may come downstairs when you have
     remembered your manners
(h) from the look of those black clouds I expect it will
     rain heavily
(i) shake the dice you have a three you have landed
     on a snake slide down to the bottom
(j) I did not try to steal that blouse I put it in my bag
     and was going to pay for it I just forgot about it
     when I left the shop

Revision exercise 6 (page 13):

Write out the following, adding only full stops and
capital letters. You should have ten sentences when
you have finished.

Stephen was very excited all day tonight he was going
out with Jane for the first time he was meeting her
outside Woolworths at seven o'clock as he went down
the High Street that evening he began to feel nervous

he was wearing his best grey suit and his favourite tie
as he came up to Woolworths he adjusted his tie it was
exactly seven o'clock he was very surprised when a
large and badly dressed girl came up to him she said
that Jane could not come but had thought Stephen
would like to take her out instead Stephen's heart sank

Revision exercise 7 (page 13):

Do as you did in revision exercise 6.

Julie was day-dreaming as she walked home when
suddenly she heard a small voice she looked down and
saw a little boy with tears running down his face he
was pointing up at the roof of an old house Julie
looked up and saw what had happened the boy's kitten
had got on to the roof and could not get down Julie
did not stop to think there was a large tree standing
beside the house and leaning over it Julie was up it in a
moment and very carefully climbed out along a branch
that almost touched the roof the kitten mewed as it
came running towards her Julie picked it up and
carefully took it back along the branch and down to the
ground

Revision exercise 8 (page 13):

Do as you did in revision exercise 6.

I am a secretary my first day at work was terrible
although now I love it I remember arriving on that first
morning it was raining my father had brought me and
because there had been an accident on our road into
town we had been delayed I was over ten minutes late
my boss was pacing up and down his office and clearly
very cross without greeting me he asked me to take
some shorthand he did not even let me take my coat off
I almost burst into tears as I sat down at the desk and
fumbled for my pencil and pad

Revision exercise 9 (page 13):

Do as you did in revision exercise 6.

the hot sun beat down on the goal-keeper he was bored the ball had been in the other team's half for almost the whole game he leaned against the goal post and watched the players at the other end of the field in a few minutes his eyes had closed and he was asleep the next thing he heard was the sound of cheering in his ears in his dreams he had made the winning save in the Cup Final he opened his eyes to see an opponent picking the ball out of his net and running back into the embracing arms of his team-mates the referee blew his whistle for the end of the game the goal-keeper's team had lost by one goal to nil

Capital letters

Revision exercise 10 (page 15):

Write out the paragraph below, using capital letters where necessary.

it is the evening of tuesday, 11th march, and the rain is falling steadily. let us take a look inside 50, meadow road, branton. this is the home of mr. and mrs. appleby and their three children. the whole family is in the living room. mr. appleby, who works for thomas banks ltd. of branton, is relaxing after a hard day. he has his shoes off and is reading his daily mirror. a glass of his favourite beer, wilson's tankard, is on the floor beside him. mrs. appleby, a large and cheerful woman, is trying to plan the family's summer holiday. on the table in front of her are several brochures from suntravel and she is trying to decide whether she would prefer a cruise in the mediterranean or two weeks in a hotel in dubrovnik. tom and lisa are watching the television. they have just had an argument over whether to watch tom's programme, crime of the century, or lisa's, lady in waiting. they are watching lady in waiting. the youngest of the family, simon, is lying on the floor surrounded by paper, plastic and glue. he is making a model ferrari racing car and hoping that his mother will forget to send him to bed.

Revision exercise 11 :

It is normal to use a capital letter at the beginning of each line of a poem, e.g.

> Jack and Jill
> Went up the hill
> To fetch a pail of water.
> Jack fell down
> And broke his crown
> And Jill came tumbling after.

Write out the following paragraphs as poems (in lines as above), remembering to begin each line with a capital letter.

(a) The man in the moon came down too soon and asked his way to Norwich. He went by the south and burnt his mouth with eating cold plum porridge.

(b) I eat my peas with honey. I've done it all my life. It makes the peas taste funny, but it keeps them on the knife.

(c) The vulture eats between his meals and that's the reason why he very, very rarely feels as well as you and I.

Question mark

Revision exercise 12 (page 17) :

Some of the sentences below are questions. They need a question mark at the end. The others are not, and so need a full stop. Write them out, adding the correct punctuation mark.

Example: *I know where you are hiding*
becomes *I know where you are hiding.*
But *Where are you hiding*
becomes *Where are you hiding?*

(a) How many legs does a spider have
(b) The Queen of Hearts wondered what had
     happened to her tarts
(c) Would you please hurry up
(d) I asked Nicholas if he would be good enough to
     stop bothering me
(e) How much did it cost to have that coat cleaned
(f) What sort of new car are you buying
(g) Why is Mr. Mappin's wife not speaking to him
(h) The pupils did not understand what the French
     teacher was saying
(i) The interviewer asked a lot of very nosy questions
(j) If there is a frost, will you be warm enough

Full stop, question mark, exclamation mark

Revision exercise 13 (page 20):

Write out the sentences below, adding the correct
punctuation mark at the end of each.

(a) How pleased we all are to see you back at school
     again
(b) The high speed at which James drove his car was
     extremely dangerous
(c) The magistrate asked the prisoner whether he
     could give any explanation of his behaviour
(d) What was the guard doing when the rebels blew
     up the bridge
(e) Were you alarmed when your spacecraft landed
     upside down and took some time to right itself in
     the heavy swell

(f)   Mercy me
(g)   Whoever did this should be severely punished
(h)   Why she did not get up when the alarm went was a
       mystery to her mother
(i)   Stick 'em up
(j)   If you knew who had stolen the tape recorder why
       did you not tell us

Comma placed between items in a list

Revision exercise 14 (page 23):

Place commas where necessary in the following
sentences.

(a)   The dingo the wallaby the kangaroo the koala bear
       and the duck-billed platypus are found only in
       Australia.
(b)   The old man coughed spluttered choked and spat
       into the gutter.
(c)   Tania's grandmother looked desperately for her
       round the shelves of the supermarket in the street
       in the car park and back in the supermarket again.
(d)   They were so determined that the expedition
       should succeed that they took with them enormous
       amounts of equipment clothing and food.
(e)   The school was a good one but its buildings were
       certainly the oldest shabbiest and most unsafe in
       the whole town.
(f)   Mrs. Sullivan loved sleeping on trains but she was
       very disappointed last time because her sleeper
       was dirty her bunk was badly made up her light did
       not work and the attendant took a long time to
       answer her bell.
(g)   Peter Piggott was soon nicknamed Porker Piggott
       because he ate loudly he ate fast he ate with his
       mouth open and he put his elbows on the table.

(h) As the pop star in the tight-fitting black suit came on stage the girls in the audience screamed clapped and even fainted in excitement.

(i) The hikers returned home wet cold dirty but happy.

(j) Jack ran straight up the middle of the field with the ball at his feet passed to his left received the return pass just in front of him and shot straight hard and high into the top left-hand corner of the goal.

Comma used to mark off a term of address

Revision exercise 15 (page 24):

Place commas where necessary in the following sentences.

(a) Mr. Chairman I should like to support the proposal put forward by Mr. Hodges.

(b) I am afraid we do not have that record in stock sir.

(c) Good evening ladies and gentlemen.

(d) Elsie you must make sure you know your tables by the end of the holiday.

(e) What made you think Miss Pilbeam that I take sugar in my coffee?

(f) Men follow me.

(g) Fetch it Fido.

(h) Operator we have been cut off.

(i) Please tell me the truth Doctor Wright.

(j) That sergeant is an order.

General exercises

Revision exercise 16:

Write out the following paragraph, using full stops or commas where the breaks (/) are shown. Use only these two punctuation marks, though you will have to add some capital letters too.

It was a lovely/warm/sunny morning and Guy was cycling down the long hill to school/he felt good/he had eaten one of his mother's best breakfasts of egg/sausage/bacon/fried bread/fried tomatoes and baked beans/it was going to be a good day at school too/in the morning he had English/games/science and current affairs and they were all subjects he liked/Guy put his head up and sniffed the air/it really was a perfect day/the next thing Guy knew was that there was a big crash/he felt himself sliding on his stomach along the roof of a car/tumbling down over the windscreen and landing with a bump on the bonnet/after a minute Guy opened his eyes/blinked and carefully slid down from the bonnet to the ground/there was a sharp pain in his left leg/he propped himself up against the large/long/old/grey saloon and looked around/he saw what had happened/cycling along with his head in the air he had not noticed the car parked beside the road and had gone straight into the back of it/luckily the roof of the car had been just the right height/Guy had gone over the handlebars/slid along the roof and bumped down on to the bonnet/he looked for his bike/there it was behind the car/Guy's heart sank/the front wheel was almost square and the handlebars were bent right back to the saddle/unhappily Guy picked it up and limped on down the hill to school/

Revision exercise 17:

Here is the punctuation for the paragraph below:

, , . , , , . . ? . ? . ? . ! ! , , . , . , . , .

These punctuation marks are in the correct order. Write out the paragraph, putting each punctuation mark in its right place. You will have to add some capital letters too.

when i was a boy i was very interested in insects
reptiles birds and all sorts of animals one wet windy
winter afternoon i went bird-watching on a flat muddy
stretch of coast the tide was coming in fast and i was
just about to leave the beach when i came across the
footmarks of a small group of animals what were they i
looked along the trail of footmarks but they soon
disappeared under the rapidly incoming tide but what
was that a few yards along the trail from where i stood i
saw a small object struggling in the mud what was it i
went quickly over to it good heavens a pig it was a tiny
shivering black piglet which had obviously been left
behind in the mud by its mother and the other piglets it
sneezed shivered and sneezed again i picked it up
wrapped it in my anorak and carried it home in the
basket of my bicycle that shivering piglet grew to be
one of the most intelligent affectionate pets i ever had

Revision exercise 18:

There is one mistake in the punctuation of each of the
following groups of words. Write out each group of
words, correcting the mistake.

(a) You are not watching this programme, you are
     going to bed.
(b) How could she possibly hope to pass her exam
     after doing no work at all!
(c) There were cups, saucers, plates, knives, and forks
     to be washed.
(d) Ann! get off my bicycle at once!
(e) Of all the subjects we do at school the one I like
     best is french.
(f) The bombers dropped over a hundred and fifty
     bombs on the arms factory. Only to find it still
     standing when the smoke cleared.
(g) Tony had just finished reading a most exciting
     story called Dr. Jekyll And Mr. Hyde.
(h) What on earth are you doing, you must not do that.

(i)   Mr. Atkins felt very, very happy as he walked to the
      station!
(j)   How easy punctuation is once you understand it?

Revision exercise 19:

Do as you did in revision exercise 18.

(a)   They made the picnic, packed the car, set off in
      great excitement, and spent most of the day in a
      traffic jam.
(b)   My dear Mrs. Boodle how good of you to come!
(c)   Jane spent two days cutting out material and
      making a beautiful dress. Only to discover she had
      made it too small.
(d)   What a very good catcher of mice Pouncer is?
(e)   Alison's favourite magazine is called sweetheart. It
      comes out on Fridays.
(f)   The jacket was a beauty, it was deep purple in
      colour and had silver buttons.
(g)   Vesuvius, Etna Erebus and Cotopaxi are all
      volcanoes.
(h)   Why do you never do what i tell you?
(i)   How many mice did Pouncer catch yesterday!
(j)   Stop crying, boy and bend over.

Revision exercise 20:

Punctuate the following paragraph, using any of the
punctuation marks you have learned in this book:
capital letters, full stop, question mark, exclamation
mark and comma.

billy it's time to get up wash your face clean your teeth
and get dressed your school trousers are on the chair
liza are you out of bed yet i woke you ten minutes ago
mr. brown will be here for you in twenty minutes and
you know he must not be kept waiting dad here's your
breakfast the paper has not come yet that was quick

billy have you cleaned your teeth your egg will be ready in a minute liza i'm not telling you again get up at once more tea dad have some toast here's your egg billy if you've finished dad go upstairs and get liza out of bed she needs a sledgehammer to wake her these days are you off billy have a good day at school

Revision exercise 21 :

Do as you did in revision exercise 20.

james hamilton slept quietly as the big plane hummed steadily through the night he was on his way back from new york to london after a fairly long very tough but finally successful business trip crack what was that over the droning of the engines all the passengers had clearly heard what sounded like a shot crack there was another the passengers were now all sitting upright wide awake and frightened the door of the first-class compartment swung open and a small dark-skinned man came through holding a revolver in the back of one of the crew slowly they came down the plane between the rows of seats as the two men passed his seat james hamilton leaped to his feet and swung his hand at the revolver it flew out of the dark man's grasp against the roof of the cabin in a few seconds the hijacker was overpowered by the passengers and led away by members of the crew james hamilton went back to his seat settled himself comfortably refused a drink from the air hostess and went back to sleep

Revision exercise 22 :

Replace each dash in the exercise below with a word so that you end up with ten sentences, correctly punctuated and making good sense. (This can be done as a class competition, either to see who can do the most in a certain time or to see who can finish first.)

Example: ____, ____ ____ ____?
could be *Elizabeth, where are you?*

(a) ____ ____ ____ ____ ____ ____.
(b) ____ ____ ____ ____ ____?
(c) ____ ____ ____!
(d) ____!
(e) ____, ____ ____ ____ ____ ____ ____.
(f) ____, ____, ____, ____ ____ ____ ____ ____ ____.
(g) ____ ____ ____ ____ ____ ____, ____ ____ ____?
(h) ____, ____ ____!
(i) ____! ____ ____ ____ ____ ____ ____ ____?
(j) ____, ____, ____ ____ ____. ____ ____ ____.

Revision exercise 23:

All the sentences below are in codes of different kinds.
Work them out and write them down in ordinary
English, correctly punctuated.

Example (this is the same code as (a) below): *OG
OTNI GNIDIH YLETAIDEMMI*
becomes *Go into hiding immediately.*

(a) EW LLAHS TEEM NI SIRAP NO YADNUS
(b) EHAV UYO DFOUN ETH ETREASUR
(c) OCOLENL EBJNMANI AHS EBNE IKLLDE
(d) REGNAD NI MA I PLEH
(e) DON OTA TTA CKL OND ONU NTI LIT ISD ARK
(f) SEK OTS NIA TPA CNO ITI SOP RUO YSI TAH W
(g) JU IBT CFFO EJTDPWFSFE UIBU DIBSMFTJT B
     TQZ
(h) RDMC LDM FTMR ZMC ZLLTMHSHNM ZS
     NMBD